The Poetic
Love
Rollercoaster

Osband Thompson II

authorHOUSE®

AuthorHouse™
1663 Liberty Drive
Bloomington, IN 47403
www.authorhouse.com
Phone: 1-800-839-8640

Published by AuthorHouse   04/12/2012

ISBN: 978-1-4685-8365-6 (sc)
ISBN: 978-1-4685-8366-3 (e)

Library of Congress Control Number: 2012906829

Dedicated To:

All of those who have loved, had their heart broken, and learned to love again. It's an exhausting battle. But it's one that's fought with good intentions. And while I've lost more battles than I've won, I continue to fight on.

—Osband Thompson II

Contents

He Wants

He wants her to be the smile on his face,
The center of his happiness.
He wants to be the pillow under her head,
The one she finds comfort in.
He wants to be the shoulder she cries on,
The support system she needs when she feels weak.
He wants to be the listener to her beautiful music,
The attentive ear to all that she has to say.
He wants to be the center of her embrace,
The kiss that her lips make contact with.
He wants her to love him.

PUSH

The lines of communication have become blurred.
There seems to be conflict with all that I say.
We can't come to a common ground.
We end up debating like Democrats and Republicans.
I keep silent to avoid yet another one sided argument.
PUSH!

Making love is close to nonexistent.
It seems to be an inconvenience to you when we come together.
We only do it when you feel you have too.
We never come together simply because you want too.
Laying there like, "Here just take it."
Turned off by your lack of interest we end up not doing it.
PUSH!! PUSH!!

My efforts go unappreciated.
I seem to always come up short in your eyes.
I love you for your strengths and weaknesses.
Yet you seem to focus solely on my faults.
We've both made sacrifices for the sake of this relationship.
Your sacrifices are held over my head and thrown in my face.
My sacrifices, while equally important, are brushed off as insignificant.
PUSH!!! PUSH!!! PUSHING ME AWAY!!!

Overrated

It's overrated.
Call me a "Hater" if you will.
But it's overrated,
And no longer lives here.
Every time I've let it reach around to give me a hug,
It's stabbed me in the back.
It's overrated I tell you.
Can't afford to keep investing in that.
It seems like the cure to all that makes you ill.
Beware of the side efforts that come from taking this pill.
I'll continue to say it's overrated,
Until you're deaf in the ears.
I'll sign language it to you,
Until you lose your sight.
Present you with a 500 page book of braille,
That will repeatedly say,
"Love Is Overrated".

Brick Wall

I used to say, "Single is safe."
There was no risk of getting hurt,
I just kept a brick wall around my heart.
But to live life without feelings,
I wouldn't be living life to the fullest.
Letting my past get the best of my future,
I would be doing myself a disservice.
It's been a long time since I've been this happy,
And I have to admit that it scares me.
Disappointments come as no surprise,
After a while you almost expect them to happen.
But I'm in pure bliss, not wanting to lose that feeling,
Praying for this happiness to be a continuous one.
The brick wall around my heart is coming down.

Lovers Bond

A soft peck on your lips,
Tongues intertwined.
Nibble on your earlobe,
Run my fingers down your spine.
Expose your breasts and caress them softly,
Taste your nipples as if they were a fine wine.
Kiss every inch of your body,
Your love box won't be forgotten.
Your toes curl, back arches, yet we have only just started.
Enter your soul, eye contact so strong.
Legs wrapped tightly around my waist,
Holding me close, our kiss is long.
Climax comes down like a thunderous nights showers.
Another soft peck on your lips.
Lay in each others arms.

1 (One)

1 worn out leather driver's seat.
1 set of keys to the house.
1 wrinkled cushion on the couch.
1 place setting at the dinner table.
1 toothbrush near the bathroom sink.
1 side of the bed slept on at night.
It appears to be such a lonely number.
1.

The Best of Me

She never had to do without,
If she wanted it, she got it,
Even if she didn't need it.
I'd put myself in debt without hesitation,
I gave her the best of me.

Yes, I was blinded by love,
Simply put, straight up naive.
But this was my life; my wife,
Never thinking she would take advantage of me.
I gave her the best of me.

Yes, you live and you learn,
I'll try not to make the same mistake again.
But after giving her the best of me,
I continue to ask myself the same question,
Do I have anything left to give?

Christmas Alone

He spends this Christmas alone.
He has two kids, two baby mommas,
Both with families of their own.
Single man, divorced, he has an empty home.
So this year he works Christmas Eve and Christmas Day,
No need to be at home with one lonesome gift under the small potted tree.
Christmas carols become his sad love songs as he looks on at happy families.
He will call his kids Christmas Day, glad they're in happy homes.
The joy in their voices will bring a little smile to his face,
At least until he hangs up the phone.
He'll watch "A Charlie Brown Christmas",
He watches it almost every year.
But this is the first time he thinks to himself,
"That pitiful looking Christmas tree is so lucky."
For at least that tree was in good company.
The day comes to a close as he leaves work to go to his empty home,
This holiday season, he spends Christmas alone.

Blood Type: LOVE+

My blood type is LOVE+.
It flows through my veins. That's how I'm built.
Love needs direction. A destination to drive towards.
I have a lot of love to give to the woman worthy of receiving it.
I luv love. I luv to love. I luv being loved in return.
Love is to beautiful not to be shared.

My blood type is LOVE+.
It's my DNA. That's how I'm built.
Love needs someone to feed off of for nourishment.
I have all the love in the world to share with that special someone.
Eventually, my lonely one will become a happy two.
Love is to beautiful not to be shared.

Another Sad Love Poem

Yes, it's another sad love poem, please bear with me.
I need to get this off my chest, it's my form of therapy.
So accept this long kiss goodbye, it's time for me to leave,
This relationship is beyond saving, therefore I'm setting you free.
No more petty arguments, taking your frustrations out on me,
While it makes yourself feel better, you fail to realize I'm not the enemy.

Yes, it's another sad love poem, please bear with me.
I need to get this off my chest, it's my form of therapy.
Be careful what you say, words can hurt more than an abusers fist,
Your words ring in my head consistently, till blood drips from my ears.
You say you didn't mean it, but I can't help but to feel you did,
Said so aggressively and well thought out, I can't help but to feel you did.

Yes, it's another sad love poem, please bear with me.
I need to get this off my chest, it's my form of therapy.
Your tongue was the third hand that slapped me across my face,
Using your words coldly, like an ice pick to my heart.
Peaceful in your mannerisms, yet you insist on going to war,
You knowingly cracked the ice before I skated over it, setting me up to fall.

Yes, it was another sad love poem, thanks bearing with me.
Glad to get it off my chest, it was good therapy.

Can You Imagine . . .

Can you imagine hating the one you love?
I must be attracted to feeling pain,
For a smart person would leave the situation.
Yet I continue to stay,
Doing my best to accept you for who you are,
Yet who you are hurts me in so many ways.
Can you imagine hating the one you love?

The BIG FISH

I am the BIG FISH.
Not an easy catch.
Not conceited or stuck on myself,
I'm just not an easy catch.
I used to be the small fish.
Took any bait dangled in my face.
Reeled me in with little effort,
Then tossed me away.

I am the BIG FISH.
Not an easy catch.
Take your time and be patient,
I'm just not an easy catch.
Don't dangle cheap bait in my face.
Reel me in with an honest effort,
I'll be the catch you'll want to keep.

I am the BIG FISH.
Would you like to catch me?

The BAIT

I'll be the top shelf BAIT,
That waits ever so patiently.
The BIG FISH will swim my way,
For I've peaked her curiosity.
She swims around me in circles,
Keeping her distance as she looks.
The reason she hasn't taken the BAIT,
Is her fear of being HOOKED.

I Need To Be Saved

"My car needs an oil change."
"Can you stop by Wal-Mart on your way home?"
I need a wife to come home too.

"I need you to pick Baby Girl up from school."
"Lil' Man has a football game you need to attend."
I need children to come home too.

I need a FAMILY.
I need to be SAVED.

There's No Poem Today

I'm sorry to disappoint you,
But there's no poem today.
The creative juices aren't flowing,
Don't want to stir up old pain.
Plus I'm lacking inspiration,
Loves possibilities not passing my way.
Scratching your head in confusion,
As you turn the page.
Cause you just read a poem titled,
"There's No Poem Today".

Your New Found Faith

". . . to be a better girlfriend, (maybe one day a good wife)."
Your new found faith in us is more beautiful than words can describe.
Without hesitation I feel comfortable with pleasing you for a lifetime.
Your smile is my Sunshine.

"We compliment each other well."
Your new found faith in us is more beautiful than words can describe.
Considering the number of struggles that we've been confronted with in life,
I feel as though God has gone out of his way to provide us with this blessing.
My hand feels empty without you holding it.
Your kiss is the air that I breathe.

"You're going to live a long healthy life with me."
Your new found faith in us is more beautiful than words can describe.
I have no fears or reservations in my commitments to you.
Your eyes keep me headed in your direction.

This Poem Is Called . . .

As I pull into the garage, it appears that they just got home themselves.
I am greeted with a kiss from Wifey and a, "Hello dad." from Baby Girl.
Baby Girl grabs an apple on her way to the living room to do her homework.
Me and Wifey take a shower together and discuss how each others day went.
We put on some comfortable sweats and head to the kitchen to prepare dinner.
"Dad, can you help me with my homework?"
I head to the living room as Wifey continues to cook dinner.
Progress is minimal. Math is my weakest subject.
"Your mom would be better off helping you with this."
As I walk into the kitchen, I say, "Baby Girl needs you."
"Math.", she replies, and we both begin to laugh.
Wifey heads into the living room as I finish preparing dinner.
Dinner is served. We come together at the table to eat.
We ask Baby Girl about school. She says she has a crush on a young boy.
Not a father's favorite topic of discussion. She's growing so fast.
Her mom encourages her to stay focused on the books and not the boys.
We know that one day she will suffer from her first broken heart.
We clean off the table and wash the dishes.
Baby Girl heads to her room to text message and call her friends.
Wifey and I sit on the couch. She lays her head in my lap.
We watch a couple of TV programs. Then we prepare for the next day.
Remind Baby Girl it's getting late, cut the phone call short and go to bed.
We all wind down and say, "Goodnight." before going to sleep.

This poem is called . . .
Family

I Continue To Search

I continue to search for
Honesty,
Loyalty,
Faithfulness.
Someone who is Trustworthy.

I continue to search for
Passion,
Affection,
Devotion.
Someone who is Lovable.

I continue to search.

Mark My Words

When you were with him, he loved you with a heavy hand,
In a relationship like that of Ike and Tina Turner,
His touch was as hard as an upper-cut to the chin.

When you were with me, I loved you with a gentle hand,
In a relationship like that of Will and Jada Pinkett-Smith,
My touch was as soft as a rose pedal against your skin.

You must love black eyes, because you went back to him.
Mark my words when I tell you, one day I'll love again,
But as for right now, me and love aren't the best of friends.

When you were with him, he was far from faithful to you,
In a relationship like that of OJ and Nicole Simpson,
He didn't hesitate to hook-up with a couple of your girlfriends.

When you were with me, I was committed 100%,
In a relationship like that of Barack and Michelle Obama,
I was the man your girlfriends wanted, but could never have.

You must love sharing your man, because you went back to him.
Mark my words when I tell you, one day I'll love again,
But as for right now, me and love aren't the best of friends.

She Knows . . .

She had my full attention when she greeted me by my name.
I greeted her back with enthusiasm as we began to conversate.
She had my mind racing, wondering how she knew my name.
I know she had done her homework, for we had never really talked until now.
She had heard my name in passing, making a point to memorize it,
First opportunity that came, she didn't hesitate to apply it.
Lips as full as a peach, and a tongue as smooth as a skater's blade on ice,
She ran me through a series of questions,
Smiling in approval with the answers I provided.
She said that until now, I always looked serious and unapproachable,
Yet it didn't seem to stop her from hunting down her prey.
A woman that knows what she wants, with an aggressive attitude to match.
Eyes as wide as a fully blossomed rose,
Piercing eye contact yearning to embrace my soul.
We exchanged phone numbers, then I proceeded to walk away,
While I may feel full right now, I will hunger for her the next day.

Accusations

Insecure, you think I want to have sex with every woman that crosses our path,
Calling me every 30 minutes, trying to account for my every move.
Analyzing my every word, waiting to hear something that doesn't sound right,
Entertaining the gossip that you hear, I'm guilty before proven innocent.
Sniffing me and my bed linens for the scent of another woman's perfume,
If I fall short of marathon sex, I must have recently had sex with someone else.

Normally, I would be livid at such accusations, but in this case, you're 75% correct.
In the past, I would have tried to cover up my dirt, but in this case, I could care less.

Miss Opportunist

Miss Opportunist is all about, "What can he do for me."
Never stopping to think about what she can do for herself,
With a hard work ethic, she could accumulate her own wealth.
Don't get me wrong, as a couple we can do this together,
But I'm not about to commit myself to a one sided effort.

"I'll cook dinner for you every night."
No need, I can do that myself,
Just call me Mr. Food Network,
I'll have you clean your plate.

"I'll keep your house clean."
No need, it's already taken care of,
I grew up a military brat,
I break out the white glove.

"I'll make love to you every night."
No need, I'll be just fine,
I discovered myself at age 11,
My hand never says, "I'm tired."

So, Miss Opportunist, don't approach me like a used car salesman,
Don't approach me with the same old lines you've used time-and-time again.
I require more than a bologna sandwich, washed dishes, and bedroom action,
I'm looking for a genuine relationship with a woman I can call my best friend.

1,000 Pieces

There are many pieces to the puzzles,
A very time consuming task,
Pay attention to detail,
So many colors, so many hues,
Most won't have the patience to complete this puzzle,
Walking away before it is complete,
This puzzle is my broken heart,
Waiting to be made whole again.

Be Warned

Love isn't welcome here,
No matter how pure your intentions may be.
I do tend to hold onto my past,
Moving forward is hard for me.
I'm doing myself a disservice,
Yes I know that's very true.
But I'm simply protecting my heart,
I suggest you do the same too.
You can try to break down this wall,
It protects my heart so dear.
Punching walls will give you bloody knuckles,
And scars that will last for years.
One of us is already hurting,
If you stick around it will become two.
You can try and win over this situation,
But I'm determined for you to lose.

Love Is . . .

Although I didn't know her, and saw her in passing,
I asked her to complete a sentence for me; to fill in the blank.
Sounds like a simple task doesn't it?
But when asked, she had to pause and think.
I told her that there was no right or wrong answer.
Then she replied with one word, "Honest."
She smiled, and as she walked away she said,
"Love is honest."

Realistic Wedding Vows

I, (name), take you, (name), to be my lawfully wedded wife,
TRANSLATION: I volunteer to take on the duty of working a thankless job.

to have and to hold from this day forward,
TRANSLATION: A marriage is like a house mortgage.
If you don't keep up with your payments, you lose your house. Your efforts are simply payments towards keeping your marriage. If you fall short, your marriage will fall under foreclosure.

for better or for worse,
TRANSLATION: During the best of times you'll be first to show up at the party.
During the worst of times you'll be the first one out the door.

for richer, for poorer,
TRANSLATION: But if you lose those riches, be prepared to lose that woman.
At least when you start out poor, there's nowhere to go but up.

in sickness and in health,
TRANSLATION: If you're sick, you can't work, and therefore don't earn a paycheck. She'll nurse you back to health, only to put you in an early grave. Before the dirt hits your casket, she'll collect the life insurance.

to love and to cherish,
TRANSLATION: Love the motto: What's mine is mine, and what's his is mine. Cherish the walk-in closet full of high heels and $500 purses.

from this day forward, until death do us part.
TRANSLATION: Her dreams and goals become yours. Yours become toilet paper. Visine tear drops at your funeral, laughter underneath her cries. She leaves the cemetery in her new BMW to shop away her pain.

Her Name Was . . .

This woman divided us.
You warned me that she wasn't a good friend to keep company with,
She would cloud my judgment and manipulate situations to benefit herself.
I let her come into our household and tear us apart,
She would show up at our doorstep uninvited and I never turned her away.
Because of her, each argument became nastier than the last.
My relationship with her became the number one priority in my life,
I became more loyal to her than I did to you.
Her name was Corona.

I spent late nights with this woman,
We partied hard together.
Be it at the club or at bars,
We partied until the sun came up.
So busy being laid up with her,
I wouldn't make it home to you until the next afternoon.
She seemed to have this hold on me,
One that would keep me away from you.
So attracted to her caramel brown skin,
The smell of her perfume.
While I continued to run the streets with her,
My true happiness was at home waiting on me.
Her name was Hennessy.

Good vs. Bad

A "Good Guy" in the beginning,
I didn't know any better.
Thinking that if I did right by a woman,
She would do right by me.
A simple minded view,
That's how things should be.
Never thinking she may feel differently,
Her intentions may not be pure.
Women can be Players just like men,
Finishing last as the Good Guy, I didn't win.

The "Bad Boy" comes out in me,
So let the games begin.
I'll treat all women the same,
Not concerned with their intentions.
Put my own needs first,
I'll assume she's doing the same.
Some of their hearts may get broken,
But who cares, so long as mine gets saved.
Previous women made me into the Player I am,
Finishing first as the Bad Boy, I get temporary wins.

I've traveled in both sets of shoes,
Struggled to see which is the best fit.
The Good Guy truly cares,
Loving his woman gives him inner wealth.
The Bad Boy could care less,
No love for a woman, only loving himself.
The Good Guy seeks quality, a life that's fulfilled,
The Bad Boy seeks quantity, feeling empty in the end.
I've gone from Good Guy, to Bad Boy, to Good Guy again.
Good Guys always finish last, but at some point have to win.

The Approach

It was a Friday night, late November, as I sipped on Hennessy and Red Bull in the club.
It never crossed my mind that I would be meeting this young lady tonight.
I was new in town, and was simply there to enjoy the environment.
I saw her across the dance floor I saw her. Standing there with a smile as big as a disco ball.
She appeared to be brushing off a guy that was desperately begging for her attention.
She continued to ignore his advances as she nodded her head to the music.
I usually don't go out of the way to approach women in this type of environment.
After all, most guys that approach women in clubs are simply looking for one night stands.
I wasn't trying to fit that stereotype. But this woman that made me curious.
I had to take my chances, at the risk of being shot down like the previous guy.
I didn't approach her with any silly lines, nor did I introduce myself with a nickname.
We talked for a nice while with unbelievably eye contact.
At one point she stepped away for a minute.
To assure me that she would be right back, she asked me to watch her purse.
When she returned, we exchanged numbers.
Not familiar with my new cell phone, she took it from me and saved her number in it.
Hoping that this gesture was genuine, and I wouldn't become a forgotten name and face,
I asked twice is she was going to really answer when I called.
Once again she assured me that she would, by giving me a kiss on the cheek,
Content at that point that she would like to go on a date in the near future.
Thinking the evening was over, she informed me that her sister had left without her.
Little did I know that she had told her sister to leave her there with me.
Her sister asked, "Are you sure you'll be safe with him, and that he won't try to rape you."
She replied, "Look at him. He's so sexy that if he wants to rape me I won't stop him."
To this day I smile at that hidden party of the story.
So, I asked her if she needed a ride home, or to a friend's house.
"No." was the reply to my question. I was at a loss for options at that point.
We're in my Jeep riding around, and I'm thinking that at I need to go home eventually.
Comfortable with me not being overly aggressive, she was cool with going to my place.
Once we arrived, I politely tried to pass the time with some conversation and drinks.
Realizing that I was clueless to her intentions, she simply said, "Let's go upstairs."
You know what happened next, or should I say, what happen three times that night.
I'm sure the next day we both looked at it as a short term fling that would pass in time.
Who would have known it would end up being a marriage.
Blessed is the day I approached her.

Bleeding Ink

Here's to another failed relationship,
If I don't laugh, I'll cry.
Truth is I'll laugh it off in front of strangers,
And shed my tears to those who I'm close too.
Friends try to cheer me up with positive words like,
"This too shall pass."
Well time seems to pass too slowly when you're in pain.
"She ain't good enough for you."
Well what does that say about me?
I don't seem to be good enough for some to love.

Please excuse my random words of confusion,
My lack of poetic structure,
My heart has been stomped on like a soda can.
So for the moment,
I'm Bleeding Ink.

I want to be sarcastic and say,
"Love is an understanding between two fools!"
I tell myself,
"Shack it off, move on, and have some self respect."
But I keep thinking,
"Has it really come to this?"
Maybe it would feel better to throw our picture across the room,
Shatter the glass in the frame.
But I'm not a violent person by nature,
So I just lay the picture face down.

Please excuse my random words of confusion,
My lack of poetic structure,
My heart has been stomped on like a soda can.
So for the moment,
I'm Bleeding Ink.

The Deepest Cut

I wasn't even aware that you were cheating on me,
Blinded by my love for you, I never thought it was necessary to look for the signs.
I got word got that you were in public with him when you were supposed to be at work.
I confronted you, and as weak as your excuse was, I believed you.
It was easier to be naive to the situation and trust you,
Rather than accept the idea that you had been deceitful.
But you continued to see this man,
And more information continued to come my way.
This man had been in our car numerous times,
This man had been in our house while I was at work one day,
This man introduced himself to me and shook my hand as if I didn't know who he was.
I gave you an opportunity to tell me what was going on, but you said,
"You know I'd never cheat. If you think that, then you have nothing else to hold onto!"
You were correct. Because that was the one thing I never doubted you one; your loyalty.
But you had to tell the truth once I told you what I knew,
At least tell what truth you wanted to admit to at the moment,
Holding back further details until you had no choice but to admit to them at a later date.
I took it as a rare moment in our relationship when you were unfaithful,
Something that wasn't in your character, therefore I didn't judge you harshly for it.
Little did I know that you had been maintaining a relationship with him,
You had even signed an apartment lease with him.
A week later, what did you tell me,
You told me that you wanted to move on with him, and that you loved him.
To tell me that you were in love with another man,
That was the deepest cut to my heart that I have ever had to endure.

You Shared

You shared something with him,
Something sacred to us,
A sexual bond,
A broken marital trust.

Not very experienced when we met,
You had only been with a few men.
Used to laying on your back and letting them do their thing.
I was the first and only person you had rode in the cowboy position,
The first person to give you oral, and the first man you gave oral too,
You learned to enjoy sex with me, it wasn't just something to do.
So, the news of another man having been with my wife has me beyond confused.
I feel like Morris Chestnut in the movie, "The Best Man",
Visions of another man helping himself to my woman.
A very secure man concerning my skills in the sexual department,
But for the first time, insecurity has started to set in.
It would be easier to imagine you simply laying on your back letting him do his thing,
But you're more experienced now, and know your likes and dislikes.
Did you tell him how you wanted it? This is what I fear.
You've never expressed to me if you liked hickeys, and he's given you two.
You love for your nipples to be sucked hard. Did you ask him to do that?
You aggressively tell me to "hit it from the back"; doggystyle,
Please don't tell me you demanded that he do the same.
Did he become the second person you rode in the cowboy position?
Was he the second person to give you oral, and the second man you gave oral too?
Please don't tell me you gave him oral, then kissed me after the fact.
When you reach your peak you repeatedly scream to me, "I'm coming",
Did you have an orgasm with him? And if so, did you let him know?
My big ego has been crushed if he was packing a larger tool than me,
I used to be the biggest that you had ever seen.
Stamina and longevity, I took pride in burning hours off the clock,
My record may have been broken, but I hope that it's not.

You shared something with him,
Something sacred to us,
A sexual bond,
A broken marital trust.

Fairy Tales Do Come True

It all sounded so sweet to her, like Cinderella, she felt like she was in a fairy tale. The possibilities seemed too good to be true. She had faith that it was possible. But it couldn't be so simple, could it?

Yes it can be so simple.
Remember, Cinderella had her hardships too.
Hardships and suffering just like you.
A fairy tale it is, just like you thought.
But when you look into a fairy tale,
They never end the way they start.
Early on there's heartache, disappointment, and immoral acts.
From our emails and discussions you've already suffered that.
No need to look back,
Look forward, I'm here.
The prince in your fairy tale.
You can wear this glass slipper without fear.

You Hate Me

I guess I've pushed you to the point of hating me,
Never have I heard that much hate in your voice,
All of which is valid.
You've been strong, taking the frustration in my voice time-after-time,
I've pushed one too many times,
So-much-so, that I don't see how you can find it in your heart to love me.
I've been so negative that you don't see any positive reason to stay with me.
My frustrations didn't give me the right to take them out on you in such a selfish manner.
While you may feel you need your space, I can't sit here and agree with you moving out,
Nor can I stop you from moving out either,
Married couples that live separately when they don't have too, usually end up divorced.
You'd be so happy to get away from me, why would you want to come back.
While you were trying to move us forward, I wasted my energy holding us back.
I can understand why these words probably carry little weight at this point,
Leaving me may be a relief for you.
I'm sorry I made you hate me.

I'm Sorry

Too much time judging you for your shortcomings,
And not enough time appreciating your efforts.
So focused on the mistakes you made,
I felt validated by deliberately making mistakes of my own.
As you continued to grow, I started to go backwards,
Becoming a person that I'm not proud of.
But you still managed to love me at my worst,
While I failed to love you at your best.
I kept holding onto the past,
Not taking the time to separate valid arguments from petty ones.
I put them all into one pot like they all carried the same weight.
I brought World War III into our household rather than peace and harmony.
Quick to point the finger at you, I didn't realize three fingers were pointing back at me.

What started off as smiles on your face have turned into frowns.
What started as laughter in your voice has turned into cries.
What started off as love in your heart has turned into pain.

I'm sorry I drained all of the smiles from your face.
I'm sorry I took all of the laughter from your voice.
I'm sorry I took all of the love from your heart.

I'm sorry that you've had to search elsewhere for smiles, laughter, and love.
I'm sorry I failed to be a good husband and friend to you.

Last In Better or End In Worse

Do you want to make visits to the tattoo parlor together; getting his and hers ink?
Do you want to go to New York Giants and Chicago Bulls games together?
Do you want to go on road trips/vacations together during long weekends/summers?
If our marriage ends in worse, we can't work towards making it last in better.
Let's fix what we've got, rather than sit back and watch it all fall apart.

Do you want me to see you get your GED, and be at your college graduation?
Do you want to be by my side when my poetry book gets published?
Do you want to be with me when you buy your first/dream car; Chevy SSR?
Do you still want to treat me to a motorcycle as a military retirement gift?
Do you want to be husband and wife when we buy our first house?
Do you want me to be there when you cut the ribbon to your own Child Care Center?
Do you want to be the person that helped me own a sports bar one day?
If our marriage ends in worse, we can't work towards making it last in better.
Let's fix what we've got, rather than sit back and watch it all fall apart.

Do you want to be a parent to my daughter and son; summer vacations together?
Do you want to be in a financial position for us to adopt your nephew one day?
Do you want us to be grandparents; celebrating our 50th Wedding Anniversary?
Do you want us to have a musical soundtrack of songs that remind us of good times?
If our marriage ends in worse, we can't work towards making it last in better.
Let's fix what we've got, rather than sit back and watch it all fall apart.

Can We?

Can I give you a goodnight kiss before we go to sleep?
Cuddle with you throughout the night, hold you close to me.
Be blessed with your smile the next morning when you awake.

Can I be the foundation in which you build your life around?
You can spread the cement as I lay the bricks.
We can make this house into a home.

Can we be what Method Man & Mary J Blige were to "All I Need"?
What Luther Vandross & Cheryl Lynn were to "If This World Were Mine"?
Help each other when one of us falls, be by their side when they stand tall.

Can you be my best friend and my future? Soulmates do exist.
Can your goals and my goals become our goals? We can play for the same team.
Can you be my Queen and I be your King? Each others pride & joy, each others trophy.

Blood, Sweat and Tears

I gave you my last name,
A name passed down from my father,
A man not born in the United States,
The last name of a man that believed in the "American Dream".
A man who became a U.S. citizen,
And volunteered to do three tours in Vietnam.
I brought you into my family,
Making you a daughter to my parents,
And a mother to my children.
I gave you my Blood.

I made my hard work ethic benefit this marriage,
Working tireless hours to provide for you,
Financially, I was invested in helping you accomplish all of your goals.
I did my best to give you a lifestyle of comfort,
So that you wouldn't have to want for nothing.
Keeping a stable roof over your head,
Food in your stomach,
Clothes on your back,
And a reliable car for you to drive was never an issue.
I gave you my Sweat.

Although I tried to stay strong when you opted to leave this marriage,
I spent many nights swimming in a pool of tears.
Slowly dragging myself out of the bed to go to work,
I tried to put on a fake smile in front of co-workers.
I doubted my self-worth,
Questioning myself as to what I did wrong,
Praying for God to bring you back to me.
I gave you my Tears.

I gave you my Blood, Sweat and Tears.

Destroy and Rebuild

Many houses that never became homes,
Just places to rest our heads.
Barbecues were few,
Hardly remember any lazy weekends in bed.
Quality time never spent in the comforts of home,
Many a silent night by yourself while I was hanging out with friends,
Followed by arguments that were usually started by me.
We built a strong foundation for this house we call a marriage,
But at some point we both made mistakes in laying the bricks,
We failed to spread the cement smoothly, thus the walls came falling down.
But when the foundation is strong, it is easier to rebuild.
The dump truck has come; it's clean-up time.
I've thrown away the broken glass and broken bricks,
All of the things in the past that have hurt me,
I pray that you will do the same.
The house has been destroyed,
Please come back and let me be the laborer,
Let me rebuild a home for you.

I Remember

I was out of town for three weeks,
We spoke on the phone every day,
It was the first time we had been apart for so long.
When I returned, you were at the airport smiling with pure joy.
High heels and a skirt that barely covered your butt cheeks,
Legs oiled up like a freshly waxed car on a showroom floor.
Breasts exposed like the sun with no clouds in sight,
With my name tattoo under the spotlight for everyone to see.
No sooner than we reached the parking lot, we climbed into the back of the Jeep,
Blanket and pillows already set up for a love session that had been long overdue,
Windows fogged up, we could care less who passed by.
And when we were finished, we laid there in the aftermath of it all.
We smiled,
We laughed,
We LOVED.

Special Thanks:

Mildred Corene Thompson: Mother. Your faith in me to succeed is unbelievable. You always remind me that you're making an investment in me. And I know you're not one to make poor investments. I always say that my mom is one of my best friends. You give me honest advice without judging me, or imposing your values on me. Thank You for keeping me in your prayers.

Osband O. Thompson: Father. R.I.P. September 17ᵗʰ, 1947-July 3ʳᵈ, 2001. Being a goal oriented person is definitely one thing I inherited from you. Never have my accomplishments reached the heights of yours. But I'm sure you're in heaven smiling, knowing that your son is a published author. Thank you for raising me into a man. Quotes that you've told have become the rule book to my life.

Daena L. Thompson: Daughter. You took a childhood love of mine, and took it to another level. Being the true definition of an artist. The days of old when we used to draw together are long gone. All I can do now is sit back and admire your skills. If this is your love, hold it close to you, and you will succeed. As far as daughters go, you've made life easy on me as a father. I take pride in your character as a young lady.

Jadan O. Thompson: Son. Proud, was I the day you finally settled in on being a loyal New York Giants fan. It's a bond me and your grandfather shared. And now it's become a bond that me and my son can share. While I may not be a perfect man, know that I make an honest effort to set a positive example of what a good upstanding man should be.

Quentin Albea: The brotherhood we share is thicker than the bond I have with some of my blood family. Although I'm a New York Knicks fan, we were like Jordan and Pippen when we used to run the streets as single men. Those were good times. You were the Best Man at my wedding; 3ʳᵈ marriage. You lent me your ear and sound advice when times were at their toughest; keeping me on level ground. Your phrase birthed the poem *Blood, Sweat and Tears*.

Greg Sutton: When I began to settle for less than the goals I set for myself, you stepped in and reminded me of what I had lost. I had lost who I was as a person. You said, "If you don't have goals to work towards, then the only thing you're doing on this earth is existing." You reminded me that I was the young guy that inspired you to be more productive with your life. I appreciate you for that.

Josie Anderton: Aside from being NFC East rivals, you're a loyal friend that roots for me just as you do for your college and pro football teams. Even when I'm wrong you've got my back. Need I say more!

Previous Relationships: No need for names to be given here. If you were in a significant relationship with me, you will know if a specific poem applies to you. There is one particular woman I would like to thank. She knows who she is. Her making me realizing the mistakes I've made in our relationship, along with the recent pain she has inflicted on my heart, gave me a wealth of inspiration to complete this book.

Printed in the United States
By Bookmasters